HUMAN HABITATS

# LUNGS

By
Robin Twiddy

Enslow
PUBLISHING

Published in 2022 by Enslow Publishing, LLC
101 W. 23rd Street, Suite 240,
New York, NY 10011

Copyright © 2022 Booklife Publishing
This edition published by arrangement with Booklife Publishing

Cataloging-in-Publication Data

Names: Twiddy, Robin.
Title: Lungs / Robin Twiddy.
Description: New York : Enslow Publishing, 2022. | Series: Human habitats | Includes glossary and index.
Identifiers: ISBN 9781978523647 (pbk.) | ISBN 9781978523661 (library bound) | ISBN 9781978523654
(6 pack) | ISBN 9781978523678 (ebook)
Subjects: LCSH: Lungs--Juvenile literature. | Human physiology--Juvenile literature.
Classification: LCC QM261.T95 2022 | DDC 612.2'4--dc23

Designer: Gareth Liddington
Editor: John Wood

Printed in the United States of America

CPSIA compliance information: Batch #CS22ENS: For further information contact Enslow Publishing, New York, New York at
1-800-542-2595

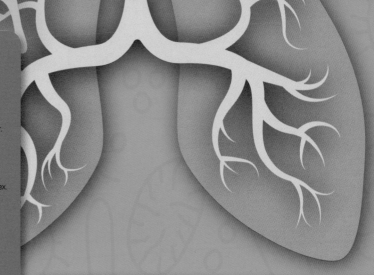

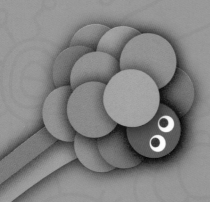

# TRICKY WORDS

Bacterium = singular
(one bacterium)
Bacteria = plural (many bacteria)
Bacterial = to do with a bacterium
or many bacteria

Fungus = singular (one fungus)
Fungi = plural (many fungi)
Fungal = to do with a fungus
or many fungi

**Photo credits:**

Cover - By Ribkhan, 4 - Iconic Bestiary, MicroOne, Fun way illustration, 6 - VectorMine, 8 - Roi and Roi, 12 - Alexey Blogoodf, Lilu330.

Images are courtesy of Shutterstock.com. With thanks to Getty Images, Thinkstock Photo, and iStockphoto.

All facts, statistics, web addresses and URLs in this book were verified as valid and accurate at time of writing.
No responsibility for any changes to external websites or references can be accepted by either the author or publisher.

# CONTENTS

Words that look like <u>this</u> can be found in the glossary on page 24.

# WELCOME TO THE HUMAN HABITAT

Hi! I'm Mini Ventura. My cameraman, Dave, and I have been shrunk down so we can make a nature documentary all about the tiny things living in and on us. Follow us into the human <u>habitat</u> — a world within a world.

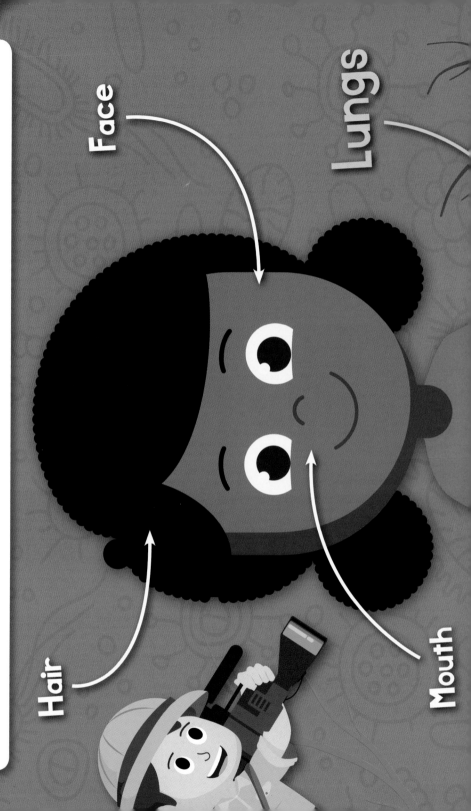

Face

Lungs

Hair

Mouth

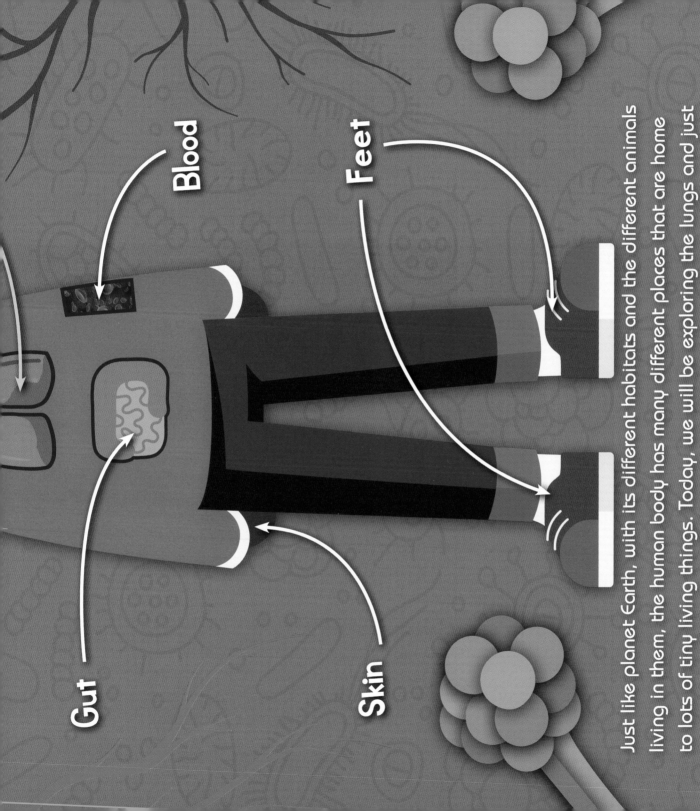

**Blood**

**Feet**

**Gut**

**Skin**

Just like planet Earth, with its different habitats and the different animals living in them, the human body has many different places that are home to lots of tiny living things. Today, we will be exploring the lungs and just a few of the things living in them.

# THE LAND OF THE LUNGS

The lungs are like a far-off land for the bacteria of the mouth. Sometimes the bacteria try to make the journey down the windpipe and into the lungs, looking for a new home.

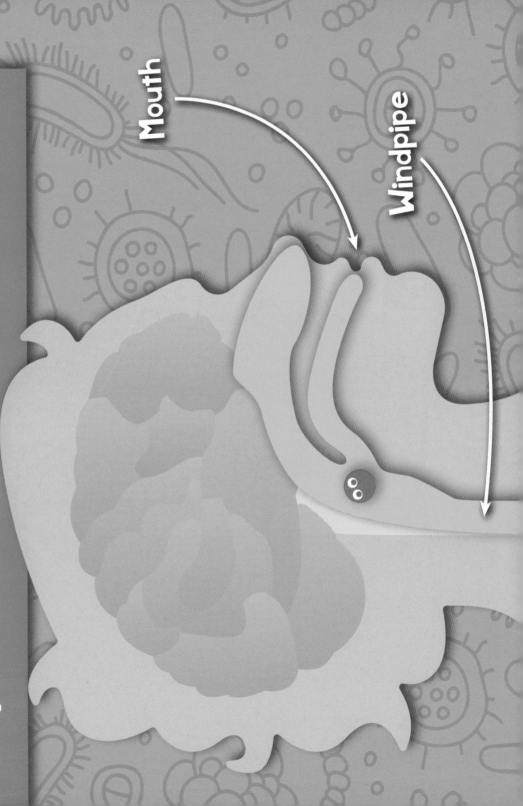

Mouth

Windpipe

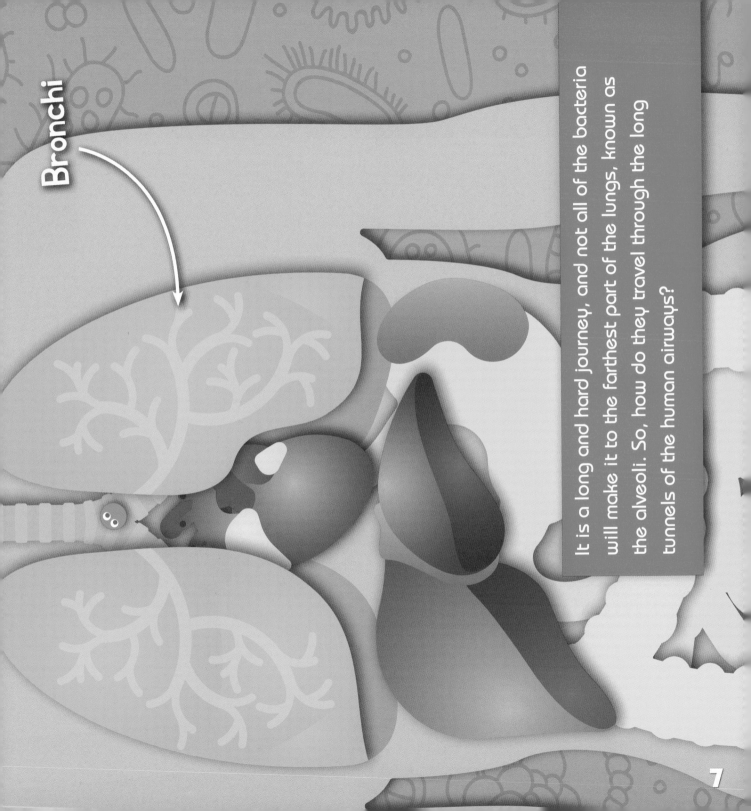

Bronchi

It is a long and hard journey, and not all of the bacteria will make it to the farthest part of the lungs, known as the alveoli. So, how do they travel through the long tunnels of the human airways?

# THE WINDPIPE

We started at the opening to the windpipe at the back of the mouth. The windpipe leads down to the bronchi inside the lungs.

Bacteria

Bacteria are so small that they can travel on tiny droplets of saliva. Saliva is another word for spit. The droplets are carried along through the airways by the breath.

Look! There go some bacteria, catching a ride on some droplets of saliva.

# THE CARINA

At the bottom of the windpipe is an area called the carina. This is where the windpipe splits off in two different directions. This is the part of the airways with the most life.

# INTO THE BRONCHI

The bronchi are tubes in the lungs. They look a bit like the trunks of trees. Thinner tubes called bronchioles split off from the bronchi like the branches of a tree.

If the bacteria want to make it to the alveoli, they are going to have to navigate these thin pathways.

Bronchi

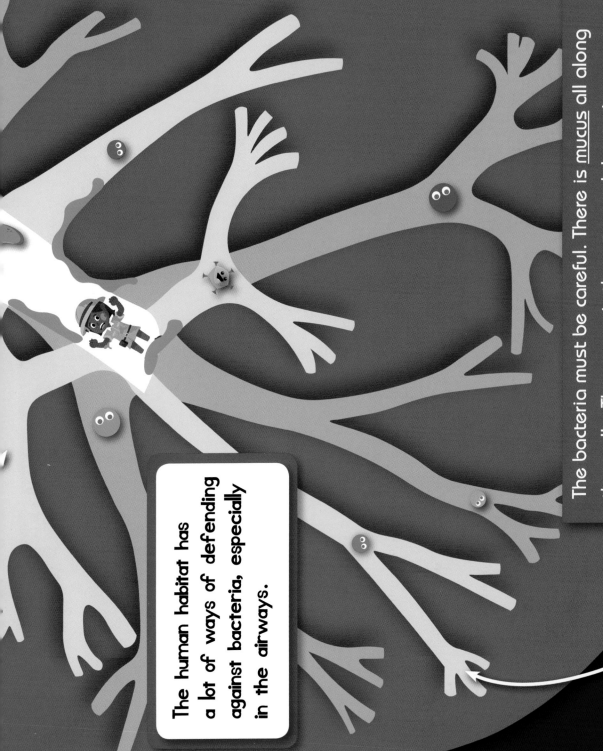

The bacteria must be careful. There is <u>mucus</u> all along the walls. The mucus is there to catch bacteria before it gets too deep into the lungs, because some bacteria can be bad for the human habitat.

The human habitat has a lot of ways of defending against bacteria, especially in the airways.

Bronchiole

# ALVEOLI

It is a long and dangerous journey, but for those bacteria lucky enough to arrive at the alveoli, the battle is not over yet.

Alveoli

If the bacteria can set up a colony (a group) here, it can cause an <u>infection</u> called <u>pneumonia</u>. If this happens, the human habitat will fight back!

The bacteria will try to make more copies of themselves and start a colony.

Colony of bacteria

# FIGHT FOR SURVIVAL

Alveolus

When an alveolus becomes infected with bacteria, the human habitat will fill the alveolus with <u>pus</u>. But this pus is no ordinary pus!

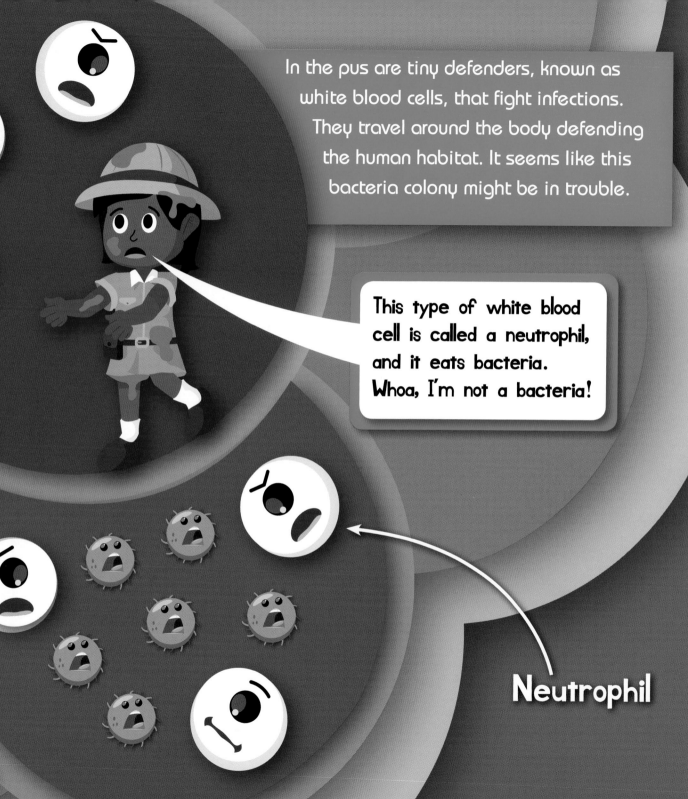

In the pus are tiny defenders, known as white blood cells, that fight infections. They travel around the body defending the human habitat. It seems like this bacteria colony might be in trouble.

This type of white blood cell is called a neutrophil, and it eats bacteria. Whoa, I'm not a bacteria!

Neutrophil

# A DANGEROUS ENVIRONMENT

If the bacteria want to make a permanent home in this alveolus, they are going to have to make more bacteria before the white blood cells hunt them all down.

It looks like this bacteria colony has failed. The neutrophil <u>predators</u> have hunted down all of the bacteria.

If the bacteria had made a new colony here, they would have damaged this alveolus and then spread to the next one.

# SURPRISE PARASITE!

Now that this alveolus has been cleaned up by the white blood cells, we should have a look in the next one. Oh dear, this is not good. We should probably go.

This looks like an infection of a fluke worm <u>parasite</u>. The human habitat will try to get rid of these eggs by pushing air out of the lungs by coughing.

# COUGH, COUGH, BYE-BYE!

It has been an exciting journey for the bacteria, even if the bacteria didn't manage to start a new colony in the lungs. Maybe the next brave bacteria will do better.

Byeeeeeeeeeeeeeee!

# GLOSSARY

| | |
|---|---|
| bacteria | tiny living things, too small to see, that can cause diseases |
| documentary | a film that looks at real facts and events |
| habitat | the natural home in which animals, plants, and other living things live |
| infection | an illness caused by dirt, germs, or bacteria getting into the body |
| mucus | a slimy substance that helps to protect and lubricate certain parts of the human body |
| navigate | to find a way around |
| parasite | a creature that lives on or in another creature |
| permanent | meant to last for a very long time |
| pneumonia | a lung infection in which the air sacs fill with pus |
| predators | animals that hunt other animals for food |
| pus | a thick yellowish or green fluid produced by the body |

# INDEX